Fundamental

GOLF

Golf instructor Peter Krause and the following athletes were photographed for this book:
Nick Berg,
Gabe Hilmoe,
Matt Hilmoe,
Sarah Hilmoe,
Angie Rizzo,
Reed Tauer,
Jenny Tollette.

Fundamental
GOLF

Peter Krause

Photographs by Andy King

Lerner Publications Company ● Minneapolis

To my parents, Mel and Kay, for their love and support and to Darrell Guay, who introduced a young boy to the wonderful game of golf.

Library of Congress Cataloging-in-Publication Data

Krause, Peter, 1954–
    Fundamental golf / by Peter Krause ; photos by Andy King.
        p.   cm. — (Fundamental sports)
    Includes bibliographical references (p.   ) and index.
    ISBN 0–8225–3454-1 :
    1. Golf—Juvenile literature. [1. Golf] I. King, Andy, ill.
II. Title. III. Series.
GV965.K69   1995
796.352—dc20   94–23166
                                                         CIP
                                                          AC

Manufactured in the United States of America

1 2 3 4 5 6 - I/HP - 00 99 98 97 96 95

The Fundamental Sports series was conceptualized by editor Julie Jensen, designed by graphic artist Michael Tacheny, and composed on a Macintosh computer by Robert Mauzy.

Photo Acknowledgments
Photographs are reproduced with the permission of: pp. 7, 9 (top), The Saint Andrew's Golf Club; p. 8, Trustees of the British Museum; p. 9 (bottom), USGA; p. 10, Rick Dole/Golden Bear International; p. 11, Dee Darden; p. 14, Nancy Smedstad/IPS, Courtesy of Tim Nelson; p. 19, Edvins Erkmanis.

All diagrams by Laura Westlund.

Contents

Chapter 1

How This Game Got Started

When you think of playing a game, what comes to your mind? Fun, excitement, challenge, competition? Without games, life would be dull. Most of the games we play require anywhere from 1 to 10 other participants. There is a game, however, that meets all these expectations, and that you can play alone or with other people. That game is golf.

Golf is played outdoors on a grass **course**. Golfers use long, slender clubs to hit a little ball across the grass into a small hole. Hitting the golf ball doesn't take a lot of strength or athletic ability. Golfers come in every size, shape, age, and skill level. The challenge of golf is that you have to think and plan your shots. And even then, there's always something new to surprise you.

This photograph, which was taken in 1888, is one of the first photographs of golf being played in the United States.

7

Paul Sandby painted this watercolor picture of golfers in 1746.

As early as A.D. 1100, Roman shepherds hit stones or feather-filled leather balls in their fields with curved sticks. This early version of golf—called paganica—eventually made its way to Scotland, where it became the game we know as golf. There are also records of golf-like games being played in Holland in the thirteenth century and in Chile in the sixteenth century.

In 1744 the Honourable Company of Edinburgh Golfers in Edinburgh, Scotland, made up the first formal rules of the game. Back then, golf was played alongside the ocean on sandy areas of land called "links." The term, **links**, is still used to describe a golf course.

The game's popularity grew with the British Empire. Wherever the British went to establish a new colony, they took their game of golf with them. Golf began in America in the original thirteen colonies.

In 1888 John Reid, an American from Scotland, asked his friend in Scotland, Tom Morris Sr., to send him a set of golf clubs. Back then, there were no factories designed to produce golf clubs. The clubs had to be made by hand. Morris was well known for the golf clubs he made. He sent a set of clubs to Reid. Reid was so happy with his new clubs that he persuaded some of his friends to try them. Morris was soon sending clubs to the United States as fast as he could make them.

This interest in the game led Reid and his friends to build the United States' first golf course, in Yonkers, New York. It consisted of three holes in a pasture. They expanded the course a few years later to six holes in an apple orchard.

In 1893 Charles MacDonald built the first 18-hole golf course in the United States. The United States Golf Association (USGA) was created in 1894 to organize and govern the fast-growing sport. The USGA sets the official rules for golf competition.

John Reid, left, helped introduce Americans to the game of golf in the late 1800s.

Theodore Havemeyer (in the straw hat) was the first president of the United States Golf Association.

Jack Nicklaus

Jack Nicklaus has won more major golf tournaments—20—than any other professional golfer. He began playing golf when he was 10 years old by tagging along with his dad. When Jack was 13, he won the Ohio State Junior Championship. Eight years later, Jack joined the Professional Golfers Association (PGA) tour.

Jack, whose nickname is the "Golden Bear," has won 70 tournaments. He has won the Masters Tournament, one of the most prestigious American tournaments, six times. He now plays on the Senior tour and designs golf courses. Jack also sometimes coaches his five children when they play.

At the turn of the century, professional golfers from Scotland and England were coming to the United States to build golf clubs and courses. Rodman Wanamaker, a department store tycoon, held a luncheon in 1916 for the top professional and amateur golfers of New York. They decided to form a national organization to promote the game and the career of golf professional. This was the birth of the Professional Golfers Association of America (PGA).

As of January 1994, there are more than 25 million golfers and more than 23,000 golf professionals in the United States. These professionals introduce new players to the game and help them develop their playing skills. Golfers can use their skills on more than 14,000 golf courses in the United States.

Some golfers play for cash prizes on professional tours. The male pros play on the PGA tour. Women professionals compete on the Ladies' Professional Golf Association (LPGA) tour, which began in 1948.

Many people play golf to relax or enjoy the fresh air. They like trying to improve their skills and master new ones. For those who want to compete against other golfers, there are high

Nancy Lopez

Nancy Lopez's father took her golfing when she was eight years old. Nancy won her first tournament the next year when she was nine, and she hasn't stopped winning since.

Nancy was born in Torrance, California, but when she was three, the Lopez family moved to Roswell, New Mexico. Nancy liked to play volleyball and basketball, dance, and do gymnastics when she was a child. But golf became her favorite sport.

When she was 16, Nancy was the top-ranked amateur golfer in the United States. Her high school didn't have a girls' golf team, but Nancy led the boys' team to two state championships. After she graduated from high school, Nancy went to Tulsa University. While at Tulsa, Nancy won the national collegiate championship.

Nancy joined the Ladies' Professional Golf Association (LPGA) tour in 1977 when she was 21 years old. She played in just six tournaments that season. In 1978 she played a full schedule of tournaments and won nine. Nancy still competes on the LPGA tour, and after winning 47 events in 16 years, she is in the LPGA Hall of Fame.

school and college teams and recreational leagues.

Whether you are playing alone or with others, playing golf will challenge your physical and mental skills. Golf fascinates many people because it pits the golfer against the course. No one is trying to tackle you, block your shot, or make you miss a pitch. It is up to you to decide how you want to hit the ball. Then you must carry out that decision. Doing that can be a challenge.

Chapter 2

Golf Shoes

Golf shoes have short steel spikes that dig into the ground and keep your feet from slipping on the grass. You can wear gym shoes, but if the tread is worn, you may slip while swinging.

BASICS

To play a round of golf you will need a set of clubs, golf balls, and shoes that are acceptable to wear on the golf course. Golf clubs are expensive. Before you spend your money, be sure you know what clubs you want to buy. Borrow clubs from a friend or relative. Nancy Lopez, a professional golfer who has won more than 40 tournaments, learned to play as a kid by using one of her mother's clubs to play the entire course. Or you can rent clubs at most courses. Ask the course pro for some clubs that fit your size and skill level. Once you are sure what kind of clubs you like—and you have saved enough money—ask the pro to help you choose clubs to buy.

Golf Balls

A golf ball weighs 1.62 ounces and is 1.68 inches in diameter. It can be constructed in one of three forms: solid piece, two piece, or three piece.

A solid-piece ball is molded out of a hard, synthetic material. This type of ball is very durable, so it is good for beginners and golfers who don't play often. This is the type of ball that is used on practice ranges.

A two-piece ball is a rubber ball surrounded by a Surlyn® cover. Surlyn is a hard plastic substance that is made by DuPont Company. This kind of ball is durable and gives the golfer good distance and control over his or her shot.

A three-piece ball is a small rubber ball that has rubber bands wrapped very tightly around it. The outer cover is a rubber material called balata. Balata is the dried sap from a West Indian tree, or the synthetic version of this sap. Professionals and very good golfers use balata balls. A balata ball will travel farther than the other balls, but it is more likely to get damaged.

All golf balls have a dimple pattern stamped into their outer cover. The dimples help control the flight of the ball by affecting the way air flows around it. The size and pattern of the dimples vary from ball to ball. The more dimples on a ball, the lower and straighter its flight will be.

Golf balls also come in different colors and have brand names with numbers stamped on them. These markings help a golfer identify the ball with which he or she is playing.

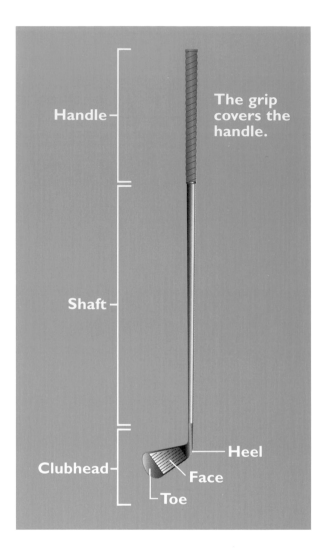

A set of clubs has at least 3 **woods,** 10 **irons,** and a **putter.** Each club has a handle, a shaft, and a clubhead. A golfer holds the club by the grip on the handle and hits the ball with the clubhead. The shaft connects the handle and clubhead.

Golf is a game of distance and direction. When you hit your first shot, you want the ball to go far and straight. Woods are the clubs designed to help you accomplish this. Woods are the longest clubs and have the biggest hitting surface. When golf began, wood was the easiest material for people to obtain and make into a club. Now, most clubs—even woods—are made of steel.

As your ball gets closer to the hole, you want the ball to go high and not too far. An iron will launch the ball high into the air so when it lands, it won't roll very far from the hole.

Once you are near the hole, you hit the ball with a putter to roll it into the cup. The putter doesn't lift the ball off the ground, but helps it roll along the putting surface.

When you look at woods and irons, you will notice a distinct difference in their design and shape. Woods have very long shafts. The clubheads on woods are shaped like half-moons. The shafts of irons are shorter than woods. An iron's clubhead looks like an open hand tilted back toward the ground.

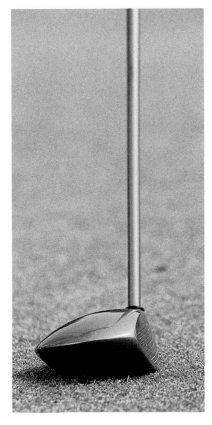
Wood

Iron

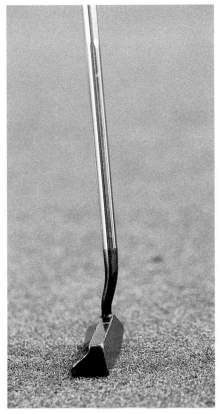
Putter

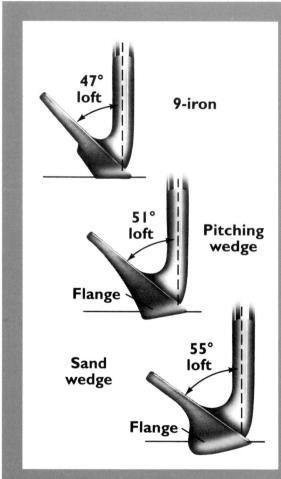

47°
loft

9-iron

51°
loft

Pitching
wedge

Flange

Sand
wedge

55°
loft

Flange

Pitching and Sand Wedges

Pitching and sand wedges have the most loft of any of the clubs. A golfer uses a pitching wedge when the ball is 100 yards or less from the hole. Using a wedge, a golfer can lob the ball high into the air over trees, sand, water, and mounds. The ball will land softly on the green and will not roll very far once it is on the green.

Sand wedges are used primarily to hit out of sand and the tall grass, or rough, around the greens. A sand wedge has a wide, flat bottom, called the flange. This slides through the sand and under the ball.

Irons have narrow channels running across the face of the clubhead. These grooves make the ball spin backwards. This back spin makes the ball stop when it lands on the grass.

When you hold an iron or wood with the clubhead touching the ground, the top of the clubhead will be tilted away from the bottom of the clubhead. This tilt is called **loft**. The amount of loft determines how high the ball will go into the air. The more loft in a club, the higher the ball will travel. To let golfers know how high and how far the ball will travel, numbers are stamped on the bottom of the clubs. Woods are numbered from 1 to 5. Irons are numbered from 1 to 10. Putters have the least amount of loft and are not numbered.

High-numbered clubs hit the ball high into the air but not very far. Low-numbered clubs hit the ball far but not high. Generally, there is a 10-yard difference between the average shot a good golfer hits with each iron and 15 yards between shots with each of the woods.

For example, a 9-iron, which has a lot of loft, will hit the ball higher into the air than a 4-iron. But the 4-iron, a longer club with less loft, will make the ball go farther than a 9-iron.

Each club's clubhead has a **toe**, a **face**, and a **heel**. When hitting a shot, you want to send the ball toward your target. The ball will fly the straightest when it is struck with the face of the

club. When a golf ball is hit properly with the center of the club face, it will spin backward as it is traveling toward the target. This helps the ball go straight toward the target.

But if the ball is hit either with the toe or heel, it will fly to the right or left of the target. If the ball is struck with the toe of the club behind the heel, the ball will spin from left to right. The ball's flight will curve to the right of a right-handed golfer; to the left for a left-handed golfer. This is called a **slice**.

If the toe of the club is in front of the heel when it hits the ball, the ball will spin from right to left. The ball's flight will curve to the left of a right-handed golfer for a **hook**.

Chapter 3

THE SWING

What makes playing golf really enjoyable is being able to hit the ball consistently toward a target. Nothing is more frustrating than swinging with all your energy and effort and watching helplessly as the ball curves away from where you wanted it to go.

In baseball and tennis, a player has to hit a moving ball. In golf, the ball stays still on the ground until it's hit. This should make things easier, but that's the tricky part of golf. By learning how to swing correctly, and then swinging that way every time, you can increase your chances of hitting the ball where you want it to go. But even then, the wind, the ground the ball is on, and the club you're using will conspire to surprise you. That is golf's challenge.

A Tiger with His Woods

Eldrick (Tiger) Woods was just 15 when he won the U.S. Junior Amateur Golf Tournament in 1991. He was the first 15-year-old to win the tournament, and the first black champion. Then, Tiger won the title the next two years to become the first three-time U.S. Junior champion.

When Tiger was 18, he won the U.S. Amateur tournament. He was the youngest winner in the tournament's history.

Home on the Range

Would you like to be able to hit shot after shot without moving from one spot? You can on a practice range. Practice ranges are designed to give golfers a chance to practice their shots. Most public courses have practice ranges. There are also practice ranges that are separate from courses. These often have practice putting greens too.

At the range, you rent a bucket of balls and then find an open space. Everyone hits in the same direction, often at targets posted at various distances from the hitting line.

The practice range is the perfect place to fine-tune your swing or experiment with a different style or a new club. It's also a fun way to keep your golf muscles in shape if you can't play a round.

Just as no two people are alike, neither are any two golf swings alike. A **swing** is determined by the golfer's height, arm length, and athletic ability. There are three elements, however, that should go into every swing: the **grip,** the **set-up,** and a mental image of the correct swing.

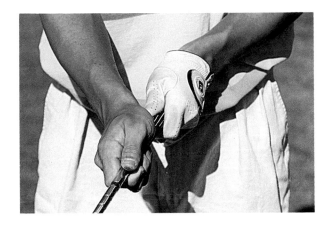

The Grip

For Nick to strike the ball with the face of the club, he must put his hands on the handle correctly. To do this, Nick thinks about squeezing the trigger of a squirt gun. Nick is right-handed, so he places the fingers of his right hand on the club where the handle and shaft meet. Then, he lifts the club up to his waist with the toe of the club pointing to the sky.

Nick brings up his left hand and "shakes hands" with the end of the handle. If you look closely, his left thumb and forefinger look like they are squeezing a trigger. He slides his right hand up the handle toward the left hand, letting his right pinky overlap his left forefinger. The rest of his hand covers up the left thumb. His right thumb and forefinger also look as if they are squeezing a trigger.

If Nick were left-handed, he would do the same thing but with the opposite hands. Using this grip, Nick can hit the ball with the face of the golf club. Variations of this grip, even small ones, will lead to shots that are struck off the toe or heel of the clubhead. Then the ball is likely to land in the rough.

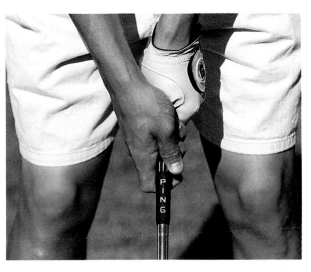

The Set-Up

To aim the club correctly, first find your target. It can be a spot by a far-off tree or bush when you're practicing. When you are playing, usually the hole will be your target. Next, think of a railroad track. Imagine that the ball is on the outside rail, on a line going to your target. Imagine that you are standing on the inside rail, with your feet, knees, hips, and shoulders all an equal distance from the outside rail.

Nick is in this position. With his club in front of his waist, Nick bends from his hips, just as if he were about to bow to someone. His knees are bent, and his weight is on the balls of his feet.

In the photograph, you can see that Nick's coach has stuck a yellow pole in the ground at the correct angle for Nick's club. Using the stick as a guide, Nick can make sure his club and body are in the correct position for his swing.

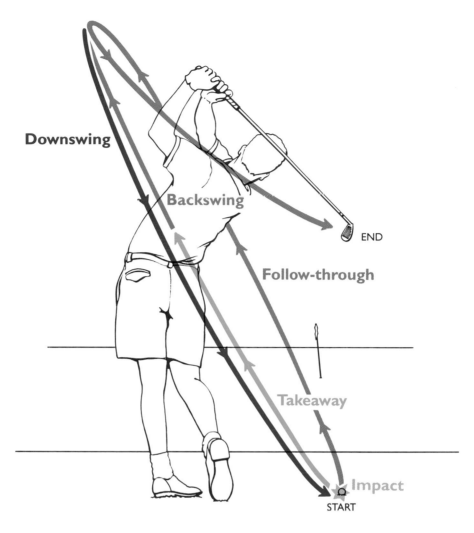

Downswing

Backswing

Follow-through

END

Takeaway

Impact

START

The Mental Image

Now that Nick is ready to swing, he gets a clear picture in his mind of a good swing. Nick visualizes a golf swing that is a combination of two motions—circular and up-and-down.

Because Nick is standing alongside the ball, his club will be swung around his body in a semi-circular motion. Since the ball is on the ground, Nick will have to swing the club in an up-and-down motion.

The trick to swinging the club correctly is mixing the right amount of each motion. When Nick correctly blends the two motions, he hits the ball with the club face facing the target. If

Nick's swing is too circular or too up-and-down, the club face will be out of position when he hits the ball.

The golf club itself helps Nick. Notice the angle at which the shaft comes out of the clubhead and up into Nick's hands. This is the angle that Nick's swing should resemble.

The Swing

There are five basic parts to a golf swing: **takeaway, backswing, downswing,** point of impact, and **follow-through.** Nick's swing will illustrate where the club needs to be in each of these positions.

The Takeaway

The most critical part of Nick's swing is the takeaway, which is when Nick moves his club away from the ball. Nick moves his hands, arms, and shoulders as a unit. At the beginning of the takeaway, the club stays in front of Nick's body as it moves up. As his arms and shoulders turn around his spine, the shaft of the club is parallel to the target when the club is parallel to the ground.

Nick can practice this move by watching his swing in a mirror. The more Nick can see himself swing the club into this position, the easier it will become for him to repeat this on the course.

The Backswing

On the backswing, Nick cocks his wrists and, at the same time, slightly turns his left forearm. This puts the club parallel to its original starting position. All the while, his shoulders are turning around his spine until his back faces the target. Nick also shifts most of his weight to his right leg. This coiling motion will supply the power he needs to hit the ball toward the target. Nick's legs should resemble a cat's, ready to pounce.

At the top of his swing, the club is parallel with the ground and the target. Nick is now ready to swing the club back down to the ball on a line that resembles the backswing.

The Downswing

"What goes up, must come down." So too with Nick's golf club. Nick's downswing must bring the club to the ball on the same path it went up.

To do this, Nick moves his hips, legs, and knees as if he were skipping a stone across a pond. This lateral movement shifts his body weight from his right leg to his left leg.

As his lower body begins its movement, Nick's hands and arms drop down in toward his right side. This puts the club at an angle parallel to the angle it was in at the set-up position. To keep the club moving toward the ball at this angle, Nick begins to uncock his wrists. This allows the club to pass through the same position that the takeaway put the club in—parallel with the target and the ground. Now the club face is in position to hit the ball.

The Swing's the Thing

To develop the proper golf swing during your practice sessions, place a golf ball 18 inches behind the ball you are going to hit. At the beginning of your stroke, swing the clubhead up and over the back ball. On the downswing, concentrate on swinging the clubhead on a path just inside of the back ball. At first try, you might hit a few shots to the right of your target. If this happens, turn your forearms a little sooner so you strike the ball with the clubhead facing the target.

The Point of Impact

At the point of impact, Nick finds out if he has swung the club correctly. The club face should be facing the target as it strikes the ball. For this to happen, the back of Nick's left hand must also be facing the target.

As the golf club approaches the ball, Nick rotates his left forearm back to its original starting position. This rotation allows the back of his left hand to face the target at impact. Also, notice how Nick's hips have turned out of the way. This allows his legs, knees, and his right foot to move toward the target, like the motion of a pitcher throwing to home plate.

The Follow-Through

For a balanced finish, Nick has to swing the club through the correct position. Just as in the takeaway, Nick swings the club after he hits the ball so that the club is parallel with the target when it is parallel with the ground. Because he has so much momentum in his swing, his arms will continue to swing up and around.

After he completes his swing, Nick's shoulders, hips, and knees are facing the target. His arms have swung across his chest, and his club is over his left shoulder. He finishes the swing with most of his weight on his left foot and his right foot up on its toe.

Even though it took several minutes to read how to swing a golf club, it only takes a couple of seconds to do it. Practice the various positions of the swing one at a time and at your own pace. But when it comes to swinging the club while playing, trust what you've worked on and believe in yourself.

Once you have learned how to swing correctly, you can hit the ball with any club—except the putter—using this swing. The club you use will determine how far the ball will travel.

Like other athletic moves, the golf swing can be as graceful and artistic as a ballerina's pirouette or a gymnast's back flip. To achieve such grace, start the club back slowly from the ball and gradually increase the speed of your swing. Swing the club as fast as possible through impact.

With time and practice, you will master the golf swing. Patience and practice are the only things you need to learn the correct fundamentals.

Iron Out a Practice Routine

The best way to start your practice sessions is to first hit with the wedge, then the 9-, 8-, and 7-irons. These short irons are the clubs that you will use when you need to hit accurate shots.

Once you are warmed up, you can hit with the longer clubs. It's always fun to see how far you can hit the ball, but trying to hit the ball hard too soon can lead to an incorrect swing.

Chapter 4

THE WAY TO PLAY

In baseball, a game lasts for nine innings and the team with the most runs at the end wins. In football, a game is divided into four quarters and the team with the most points wins. Golf is different.

The Course

Golfers try to use the fewest possible **strokes** to hit a ball into a small opening in the ground. Both the opening and the area of the course you play on before reaching it are called a **hole**. A golf course has 9 or 18 of these holes, separated by yards of grass. The golfers play each hole in order. There is no set time limit for a golfer to play a hole. Eighteen holes make up a complete game, known as a **round**. The term round came from the early golf courses built in Scotland. Many were laid out in a circle with the starting and finishing points near each other.

Getting Better

If you want to become a better golfer, you have several options. The professionals at most courses teach private lessons. Ask the pro at a course near you if he or she teaches young golfers and what the fee is.

Many community education programs and recreation centers offer golf classes or group lessons. Check with the physical education teacher at your school.

There are also golf camps, just like hockey or basketball camps, that advertise in golfing magazines. Check around for the camp that sounds right for you. Or, stay home and borrow instructional videos from the library or video store. And don't forget to practice!

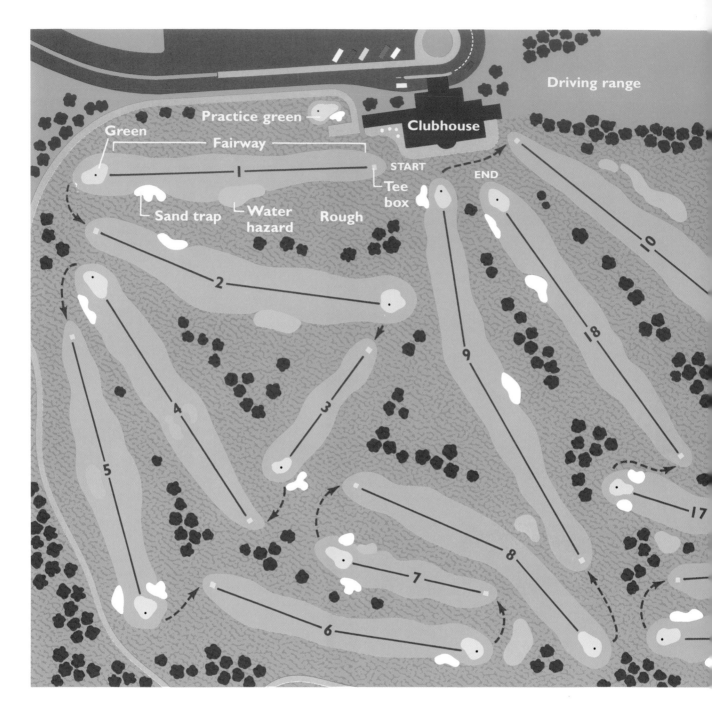

Each hole is made up of a **tee box**, a **fairway, rough, hazards,** and a **green**. The tee box is where you begin to play a hole. The tee box is defined by two markers. The ball must be hit between the two markers. Often there are three sets of markers. Women hit from the red markers, men hit from the white markers, and professionals or tournament players hit from the blue markers.

You are allowed to hit your first ball off a 2-inch wooden peg called a **tee**. All other shots on the hole are played off of the ground. On the next hole, you may start play with a tee, or tee off, again. The shot you hit off the tee is also called a **drive**.

The fairway is an area of grass that extends between the tee box and the green. The grass is cut to a height of

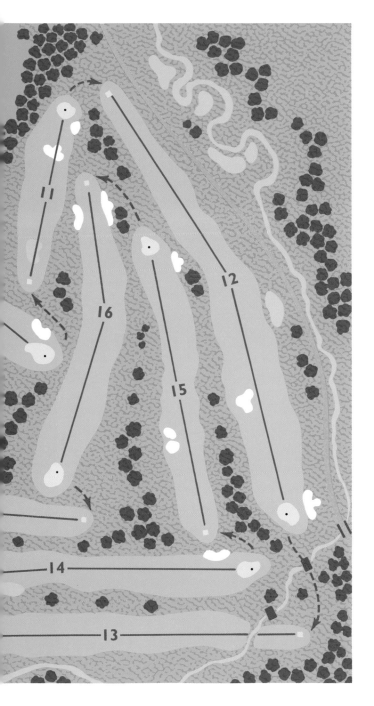

traps. Hazards are designed to make playing more difficult. Water hazards are marked with red or yellow poles.

The green is an area of grass that is cut shorter than the fairway grass. This is where the **cup** can be found. The cup is 4¼ inches in diameter and 4 inches deep. There is a removable 6-foot pole with a flag on top of it in the cup. This **flagstick,** or **pin,** shows golfers where the cup is on the green. Once you have hit your ball into the cup, you are done with that hole. Your score is the number of times you hit the ball.

Scoring

Holes generally vary in length from 100 to 600 yards. A skilled golfer should be

only 1 to 2 inches. The rough surrounds the fairway. The grass in the rough is 3 to 6 inches high. There also may be bushes and trees in the rough. An area is **out of bounds** if play isn't allowed there. An out-of-bounds area may look like the rough but it is usually marked by a sign or white poles. Hazards are ponds, streams, and large, shallow holes that are filled with sand and called sand

Golf's Handicap System

Not everyone who plays golf has the skills to shoot par. To allow people of various skill levels to compete against one another, a handicap system is used. A **handicap** *is the average number of strokes a golfer shoots over par. This number is subtracted from the golfer's actual score.*

For instance, let's say John usually shoots a score of 95 for 18 holes. His average score is 23 shots higher than par, so his handicap is 23. If John shot a 93 for 18 holes, he would subtract 23 from his score for a net score of 70. This means he beat the par-72 course by two shots. Handicaps range from 0 to 36. A golfer's handicap is based on his or her skill level and the difficulty of the course he or she is playing. Golfers turn in their scorecards to the course professional after playing a round. These scores are recorded, and their handicaps are figured.

able to play each hole in a certain number of strokes. Holes that are less than 250 yards long are expected to be played in three shots. Holes that are 250 to 475 yards are meant to be played in four strokes. Holes longer than 475 yards are supposed to be played in five shots.

The expected number of strokes is called **par**. You measure your score against par. If you use that many strokes to play a hole, you have shot par, or parred the hole. If you play a hole with one stroke less than par, you have shot a **birdie**. Two shots better than par is called an **eagle**. When you take one stroke more than par, you have shot a **bogey**. Two shots over par is a double bogey, and three shots over par is a triple bogey, and so on.

The par number always includes two putts. For example, a par-3 hole means that a top-notch golfer is expected to hit his or her tee shot to the green and putt twice to finish the hole. On a par-5 hole, that talented golfer is supposed to take three shots to get the ball on the green before putting twice.

A typical golf course has 4 par-3 holes, 4 par-5 holes and 10 par-4 holes. The 18 pars add up to 72. So, the goal is to shoot a score lower than 72.

Of course, when you are learning to play you will have different goals. Maybe you will want to keep your score on each hole to 10 or better. Maybe you will try to keep your total score under 120. Shooting par is a challenge for all golfers but the very best. Don't get discouraged if par seems a long way off. Just try to do your best, one shot at a time, and see if you can keep improving.

Rules and Etiquette

Like other sports, golf has rules and regulations. When a player breaks a rule, a shot is added to his or her score as a penalty. For example, Angie has hit her ball into the water and is unable to play the shot. She must take a penalty of one shot. She can either re-trieve her ball from the water or, if the ball is too far in the pond to recover, she can use a new ball. Angie drops the ball within one club length of where her shot went into the water.

Sarah has a different problem. Her ball is up against a tree and she can't hit it. She must take a penalty of one shot to move her ball away from the tree (but not closer to the cup). Golf is unlike other sports because the player, not an umpire, decides that a rule has been broken. That's why golf is a great game for developing your character!

Golf also has its own special set of manners, or etiquette. Be quiet and still while others are making their shots.

Don't walk between the cup and another player's ball on the green. Congratulate a player on a good shot, but don't offer advice after a bad one. If there's any chance your ball could hit a person playing in front of you, don't swing. If, after you've hit your ball, you see someone who could get hit by it, yell "Fore!" That warns other golfers that a ball in flight might hit them.

The rules of golf allow up to four people to play a hole at one time. The person with the lowest score on the previous hole is the first one to tee off on the next hole. (You can flip a coin to see who hits first on the No. 1 tee box.) While playing a hole, the person whose ball is farthest from the cup hits first. This order of play is followed until the hole is completed by all players. Keep track of where your companions are on the hole so you are ready to hit when it is your turn.

There is no time limit in golf, but golf etiquette calls for golfers to keep their game moving along. It usually takes four hours to play 18 holes of golf. This is a long time when many people want to play. Don't rush your shots, but don't dawdle between shots. Always be ready when it is your turn to play. Watch your ball and those of your partners. If a ball goes into the rough, try to notice something, like an oddly shaped tree or a bend in the fairway, near where you last saw the ball. Using that marker, you can find the ball without a long search.

When playing a round of golf, keep pace with the group in front of yours. If you are falling behind or if you've lost a ball, allow the group behind you to "play through" your group. Let that

Marking Your Putt

Once you are on the green, you may find that your ball is between another golfer's ball and the cup. Then, according to the rules of golf, you must move it. You are also allowed to pick up your ball and clean it off before putting.

Before you pick up your ball, slide a coin behind the ball to mark your position. Then pick up the ball and clean it. When you are ready to putt, replace the ball and pick up the coin.

group tee off on the next hole before your group does. Or, when on the green of a par-3 hole, wave so that the golfers behind you know that they can hit their shots onto the green. Then, allow them to finish the hole before you complete your play.

Learning to play quickly can be beneficial, especially in a tournament. In a tournament, an official times every golfer's play. If the official decides you are playing too slowly, he or she will add two shots to your final score. Even when you're not in a tournament, playing slowly might aggravate the players in your group and those playing behind you.

Chapter 5

SKILL SHOTS

There is more to golf than full swings. Some of the skill shots, such as chipping and pitching, use the full golf swing as a starting point. But putting demands different skills. Learning these advanced shots takes time and effort. Mastering them will make you a good golfer.

Chips

When a golfer is within 10 feet of the green, he or she will hit a short, low shot called a **chip**. The object is to hit the ball out of the long grass and just onto the green. Once on the green, the ball will roll like a putt. You want the ball to finish as near to the cup as possible. With a good chip, you'll only need one putt to sink the ball in the cup. You can use a 7-, 8-, or 9-iron to chip.

To execute the shot, Matt places his grip farther down the handle than he would for a full swing and leans his body and club toward the cup. He imagines his hands, arms, and shoulders are a pendulum. He strikes the ball with this pendular motion. There is very little follow-through on a chip, so Matt's club stops soon after he hits the ball. The ball pops up into the air and lands on the green.

Pitch Shots

Often you will find yourself in situations where there is a sand trap, or **bunker,** between you and the hole. A chip shot would not work in this case because the ball would not roll through the sand. You need to hit a shot that flies over the bunker, lands on the green and doesn't roll very far. This is called a **pitch** shot.

A pitch shot makes the ball fly farther in the air than it will roll on the ground. The shot looks like the path of a pitched horseshoe. When the ball is lofted in the air, it will not have enough momentum to roll like a chip would.

Gabe is using a 10-iron to hit a pitch shot. His grip is toward the bottom of the handle. He is aiming the clubhead

at his target. His body and club are leaning slightly toward the cup.

Gabe moves the club back from the ball with a slight cocking of his wrists. As he starts his downswing, his knees move toward the target. Meanwhile, his wrists uncock toward the ball. When he hits the ball, the loft of the club makes the ball go up.

Gabe swings the club well past the point of impact for a full follow-through. The ball flies high into the air and lands softly on the green.

Putts

Putting occurs on the closely mown area of the golf course called the green. The surface of the green resembles the felt covering on a pool table. Putting is very challenging because the green is not flat. A green has miniature slopes and hills that will cause the ball to roll on curved paths.

When putting, you must judge how hard to hit the ball and what path the ball should take to the cup. The slower the ball rolls, the more it curves because of the slope. For example, Matt is 20 feet from the hole. The green he is on has a 2-foot slope from right to left. Matt has to start the ball rolling 2 feet to the right of the cup with the proper speed to make it go in.

Reading the Green

The key in determining how much a putt will curve is noticing how much slope there is in the green and deciding how hard you must hit the ball. Which end of the green is higher than the rest? The ball will always curve away from the highest point. The speed of the putt will determine how straight it will roll. The faster the ball rolls, the straighter it goes.

There are many different putting styles, just as there are many different full swings. But a putting stroke should be very simple, much simpler than a full swing.

Jenny is holding the handle. Notice how both of her thumbs are pointing down at the clubhead. She has aimed the clubhead on the path she wants the ball to start rolling.

As she swings the putter, Jenny imagines her hands, arms, and shoulders are a pendulum. This pendular motion makes the putter move straight back from the ball and straight to it. With practice, Jenny has learned how hard to hit her putts.

Practice Putts

Here's a drill that will help you learn how hard you should hit your putts. Take five golf balls and line them up in a row. Take five steps from the balls and by each step, place a tee in the ground.

Go back to the row of balls and try to hit the first ball to the first tee. Then hit the second ball to the second tee, and repeat this with the rest of the golf balls. Practice this drill from 10, 15, and even 20 steps.

When you are on the golf course, count your steps from the ball to the hole. Now remember your practice sessions and hit the ball just hard enough to make the putt.

Bunker Shots

Bunkers, or sand traps, are often found alongside a green. If you hit your ball into a bunker, be sure not to let your club rest on the sand before you begin your stroke. A penalty stroke is assessed if your club touches the sand before you swing to hit the ball. Start your shot with the clubhead at least 1 inch above the sand.

The object of the shot is to hit the sand 2 inches behind the ball and allow the club to slide underneath the ball. The buildup of sand between the ball and clubhead propels the ball out of the bunker and onto the green.

If possible, use a sand wedge to play a shot out of the bunker. The sand wedge is designed to get the ball out of the sand. The bottom of a sand wedge is lower than other iron bottoms. This allows the clubhead to slide through the sand. If you don't have a sand wedge, use a 9-iron or pitching wedge.

Reed starts his bunker shot with the proper grip. He digs his feet into the sand to keep his balance. His feet are pointed toward the left of the cup. Reed aims the clubhead at the cup.

Reed swings as he would for any other full swing. He swings very hard because he will hit sand instead of the ball. Reed follows through so that the sand doesn't slow the clubhead. The ball floats out of the bunker and lands softly on the green.

Chapter 6

Warming Up

Before you play any sport, including golf, you need to stretch and warm-up. One simple stretching exercise is to place a club behind your back and between your elbows. Spread your feet shoulder width apart and start turning to your right and back to your left.

Then place the club behind your back across the shoulder blades and repeat the same twisting motion. Finally, hold the club in front of your waist, bend from your waist and touch the ground. In just a few minutes, your muscles are stretched and ready to swing the club.

ON THE COURSE

Learning the proper swing techniques and various shots will take plenty of practice. Keep in mind, however, that the practice will help you shoot a low score. It also prepares you for the challenges that are waiting for you on the golf course. When playing, you must manage the wind, avoid the sand and water, and deal with the pressure of putting. Let's see how the foursome of Nick, Reed, Sarah, and Jenny put this practice into action.

They are about to play a par-4 hole that is 385 yards long. Golf courses have men's tee boxes and women's tee boxes. Because most women don't hit

Hole In One!

*When a golfer hits the ball into the cup with only one stroke, he or she has hit a **hole in one**. A hole in one is rare! A golfer needs skill to be able to hit the ball so accurately that it goes in with one shot, but most golfers would agree that luck is the main ingredient of this great feat. Holes in one occur primarily on par-3 holes, but they have also been made on par-4s. A hole in one on a par-3 is called an eagle. On a par-4, it is called a double eagle.*

the ball as far as most men, the women's tee boxes are closer to the hole. Jenny and Sarah will start playing from the women's tee box. Nick and Reed will tee off first because their tee box is farther from the hole.

As Nick prepares for his tee shot, his eye catches the sand bunker to the left of the fairway and the trees to the right of it. He feels the wind blowing from right to left and instinctively plans to hit the ball down the right side of the fairway. He places his hands firmly on the handle and positions his body and clubhead to the right of the fairway. The club moves slowly back from the ball, gradually building up speed to launch the ball down the fairway. The ball explodes off the club face and blasts down the right side of the fairway. Nick watches as the wind blows the ball to the left. It lands in the middle of the fairway. Jenny turns and says, "Nice shot!"

Next Reed bends down and puts his ball on a brand-new white tee. He steps back and swings his No. 1 wood, or driver, several times. As he steps up to the ball, he wiggles the club to get comfortable. Reed slowly brings back the driver, then whips it down to hit the ball. The ball flies off the tee, which shatters at the impact. Reed's spirits sink as he and Nick watch the ball's flight. The small white spot curves to the right, slicing into the rough.

Now it's Sarah's turn. She takes a couple of practice swings by the women's tee while she pictures the flight of her ball down the middle of the fairway. Sarah carefully positions the clubhead and her body to execute a smooth, fluid swing. Her efforts are rewarded with a long, straight drive.

Jenny is the last to tee off. After several practice swings, she gets into her set-up position. She takes a deep breath, blows it out, and begins her takeaway. Whipping the club to the ball, Jenny drives the ball forcefully off the tee. But when she looks up, Jenny sees that she too has landed in the rough to the right of the fairway.

"C'mon Jen," Reed calls as he slings his bag of clubs over his shoulder. "You can keep me company. At least you didn't slice it as bad as I did."

Nick and Sarah walk down the fairway and begin preparing for their second shots. As they approach their tee shots, they look to see where their balls are in relation to the 150-yard marker. Many golf courses have plates on the fairway indicating how far you are from the green. Sarah's ball is 160 yards from the hole and Nick's is 145 yards away.

Divot Duty

When hitting a shot with an iron on the fairway, quite often your clubhead will tear out some turf. This chunk of earth is called a **divot***.*

If the divot came from the ground ahead of where your ball was, you're hitting the ball correctly. If the divot came out before you hit the ball, you goofed. Your swing loses a lot of power if the club hits the ground before it hits the ball. Often this happens if you are trying to scoop up the ball or lift it into the air. Remember, the club's loft is designed to do this for you. Just relax, take a deep breath, and try to swing the club smoothly.

But first, replace the turf that you dug up. Simply place the divot back in the ground and step on it with your foot. This gives the grass a chance to grow and keeps the fairways clean.

Jenny finds her ball among some small trees. Her ball is about even with Sarah's, but because it curved to the right, it's farther from the hole. Reed, meanwhile, finds his ball even farther to the right than Jenny's, but 20 yards closer to the hole than Nick's ball. Jenny will hit first.

Jenny decides to hit a 7-iron. She wants to hit the ball high and far so it can clear the sand bunker in front of

the green. Jenny swings and hits the ball solidly, but her troubles continue. The wind blows her ball into the bunker. "Tough luck Jen," Sarah calls from the fairway. "But you're good in the sand!"

Sarah closes her eyes for a moment and pictures the 7-iron shot she wants to hit. Then she steps up to the ball, takes a deep breath, and swings. It's a beautiful shot, heading straight for the pin. The ball lands on the fairway, just a couple of yards in front of the green. "Nice shot Sarah! You're hot today!" Jenny says, walking up to her friend.

Nick chooses to use his 9-iron for his second shot. His strong, balanced swing produces a solid shot. He looks up to see his ball tracking down the flagstick like a guided missile. The ball lands softly on the green, and rolls until it is just 15 feet from the cup.

Jenny, Sarah, and Nick walk down the fairway, keeping their eyes on Reed. He's ready to hit his shot now that they've hit theirs. Reed's ball is nestled in some tall, thick grass in the rough. To power it out of the grass, he picks his 9-iron. Reed's swing is solid, but the ball is held up by the wind and lands in the bunker, just 5 feet from Jenny's. "You don't have to keep me company, Reed," Jenny teases. "Didn't want you to get lonely," is Reed's answer. Nick chimes in, "I'm the one who's lonely, all by myself on the green," and Sarah throws a golf towel at him.

Jenny walks into the bunker holding her sand iron. She carefully digs her feet into the sand to avoid losing her balance while she swings. To avoid the penalty, Jenny doesn't let the clubhead touch the sand before she swings. Jenny's swing slides the clubhead underneath the ball. The force of her swing produces a shower of sand, and the ball comes flying out. She eagerly watches her ball land on the green and roll to within 3 feet of the cup. She heaves a big sigh of relief as Reed yells, "Great shot! Hope I can do that."

Reed walks out onto the sand and wiggles his feet into a comfortable stance. "Keep your fingers crossed," he says to his friends. His shot also comes blasting out of the bunker in a spray of sand, but his ball rolls past the cup and about 20 feet down a slope. "At least you're out of there," Sarah says as Reed rakes the sand.

While Jenny and Reed were blasting out of the bunker, Sarah was studying her shot. She wants a chip shot that will land and roll to the cup. She swings

Minding Your Business in a Bunker

After you have hit a sand shot, you will notice that your feet and club have made quite an impression in the sand. It is common courtesy to grab a rake, which should be alongside the bunker, and rake the sand until the surface is smooth again.

her 9-iron and gently launches the ball. It lands about 20 feet from the cup. The ball rolls down a small slope to within 10 feet of the cup.

Reed will putt first. Since Jenny's ball is the closest to the hole, she pulls the flagstick from the cup and lays it down on the edge of the green. She's careful to keep it out of the way of any of the putts.

Reed was studying the uphill slope he faces while Sarah was chipping on the green. Now he stands over the ball and strokes a few practice putts. He aims for the right of the cup and strokes the ball firmly, but not too hard. Reed's ball climbs up the slope and

curves to the left, but rolls to a stop 2 feet short of the cup.

Nick was carefully surveying the slope of the green as Reed putted. He was trying to imagine how the ball would roll off the slope and into the cup. As he crouches behind the ball,

Nick notices that the slope of the green is from his left to his right. He decides he must start the ball rolling about 6 inches to the left of the cup.

Nick walks up to the ball and takes two practice strokes, all the while thinking about how hard he should swing the putter. He carefully aims the club and gently swings the putter. The ball starts rolling on the path he had chosen. Nick gets worried. Did I hit it too hard? Is it going to curve in or not? Then he hears the gentle "plop" of the ball falling into the metal cup. A birdie! A big smile spreads across his face. He has beaten the hole by using one stroke less than par. "Wow, way to go Nick!" "Nice shot buddy!" Nick grins as his friends congratulate him.

"OK, Sarah, sink this one," Nick says as Sarah steps up to her ball. She has a 10-foot putt, but she thinks it's a straight-on shot. She bends over the ball, slowly draws back her putter, and taps the ball. Sarah holds her breath as her ball heads straight for the hole, catches the lip of the cup, and bounces just inches from it. "Tough break!"

Jenny faces a 3-foot putt up the slope. She thinks that the slope is not going to make the ball curve. She pictures the ball rolling into the hole as she practices her stroke. Her stroke is

firm and smooth, the ball comes off the putter and rolls right into the center of the cup. She picks her ball out of the hole as Nick congratulates her for saving par.

Then Reed steps up for his second putt. This time the ball is about 2 feet from the cup. He taps the ball, gently but firmly, and sighs with relief as it falls into the cup. "OK Sarah, finish it off," he says as he picks up the flagstick. Sarah taps in her ball from 6 inches away, and Reed replaces the flagstick.

The four friends step away from the green so that the players behind them can hit onto the green. But before going on to the next hole, they pause to record their scores. "You're the bogey man, Reed," Nick says. "Oh yeah, well just watch me on this hole. I love these par-5s," Reed says, smiling. "I'm staying out of trouble on this one," Jenny vows. "No rough and no sand for me!"

If you want to test your abilities—like Reed, Nick, Jenny, and Sarah—pick up a club and head for the golf course or the practice range. With blue sky above you and green grass beneath your feet, you'll discover how challenging and fun playing golf can be.

GOLF TALK

backswing: The motion of the golfer and club that brings the club away from the ball and up.

birdie: A score that is one stroke less than par.

bogey: A score that is one stroke more than par.

bunker: A depression in a fairway or next to a green that is filled with sand.

chip: A short, low shot that is made from close to the green. The golfer intends for the ball to roll across the green after it lands.

course: A series of holes, usually 18 but sometimes 9, that are laid out over a grassy area. The holes are numbered consecutively.

cup: The 4¼-inch hole on a green into which the ball is hit.

divot: A piece of turf that is dug up by a clubhead during a swing.

downswing: The motion of the golfer and club that brings the club down and toward the ball.

drive: The first shot hit by a golfer on each hole.

eagle: A score that is two shots less than par.

face: The surface of the clubhead that strikes the ball.

fairway: The area between the tee box and the green that is designed to be played on. The grass on the fairway is cut shorter than the rough but not as short as the grass on the green.

follow-through: The motion of the golfer and club that completes a swing after the ball has been hit.

green: A smooth area around the cup where the grass is cut very short.

grip: The way a golfer holds a club. Also, the portion of a club a golfer holds.

handicap: The average number of strokes over par a golfer plays. This number is subtracted from that player's score when he or she is competing.

hazard: An obstacle on the course designed to make playing more difficult, such as a bunker or pond.

heel: The portion of the club that joins the shaft to the clubhead.

hole: An area of a course, defined at the start by the tee box and at the finish by the green, over which a golfer hits the ball. Also, the cup on a green.

hole in one: A first stroke on a hole that knocks the ball in the cup.

hook: A shot that curves from right to left in the air.

iron: A club with a thin metal head and a grooved face that is tilted.

links: Originally a course on sandy strips of land between the ocean and the mainland. Now links is a nickname for any course.

loft: The angle between a club's shaft and clubhead. The greater the angle, the higher the ball will fly.

out of bounds: An area next to or on the course on which play is not allowed.

par: The number of strokes a golfer is expected to use to complete a hole. Par is set for each hole, depending on its length.

penalty stroke: A stroke added to a player's score when that player has broken a rule.

pin: A slender 6-foot pole with a flag at the top. A pin is stuck in each cup to show golfers the cup's location. Also called a **flagstick.**

pitch: A short, high shot, usually hit over water or a bunker. The golfer intends for the ball to stay where it lands on the green and not to roll.

putt: A stroke used when on the green that is designed to roll the ball toward the cup.

putter: A club with a long, flat hitting surface that starts the ball rolling on the green.

rough: The area on a course where grass and weeds aren't mowed. Often there are bushes and trees in the rough also.

round: A complete game of golf (18 holes).

set-up: The position a golfer assumes before hitting the ball.

slice: A shot that curves from left to right.

stroke: The motion a golfer uses to hit the ball. Also called a **swing.**

takeaway: The early part of the backswing during which the club is pulled back away from the ball.

tee: A small wooden or plastic peg on which the ball is placed before the first shot of a hole.

tee box: The marked area at the start of a hole from which a golfer's first shot is hit.

toe: The part of the clubhead farthest from the shaft.

wood: A club with a large clubhead and a flat hitting surface.

FURTHER READING

Lopez, Nancy. *Nancy Lopez's The Complete Golfer.* Chicago, Illinois: Contemporary Books, Inc., 1987.

McCormick, Bill. *The Complete Beginner's Guide to Golf.* New York: Doubleday & Company, Inc., 1974.

Mulvoy, Mark. *Sports Illustrated Golf.* New York: Harper & Row, Publishers, 1983.

Wiren, Gary. *The PGA Manual of Golf.* New York: Macmillan Publishing Company, 1991.

FOR MORE INFORMATION

American Junior Golf Association
2415 Steeplechase Lane
Roswell, GA 30076

Hook A Kid On Golf
2611 Old Okeechobee Road
West Palm Beach, FL 33409

Ladies' Professional Golf Association
2570 Volusia Avenue, Suite B
Daytona Beach, FL 32114

Professional Golfers Association of
   America
100 Avenue of the Champions
PO Box 109601
Palm Beach Gardens, FL 33410

United States Golf Association
Liberty Corner Road
Far Hills, NJ 07931

INDEX

Madison County Library
P O Box 38 1315 Hwy 98 West
Danielsville, GA 30633
(706)795-5597
Member: Athens Regional Library System